Oklahoma Department of Libraries

)avis

..nales

Celeste Didlick-Davis

Reentry Experiences of Formerly Incarcerated Females

Personal Perspectives from Females Returning Home

LAP LAMBERT Academic Publishing

Impressum / Imprint

Bibliografische Information der Deutschen Nationalbibliothek: Die Deutsche Nationalbibliothek verzeichnet diese Publikation in der Deutschen Nationalbibliografie; detaillierte bibliografische Daten sind im Internet über http://dnb.d-nb.de abrufbar.

Alle in diesem Buch genannten Marken und Produktnamen unterliegen warenzeichen-, marken- oder patentrechtlichem Schutz bzw. sind Warenzeichen oder eingetragene Warenzeichen der jeweiligen Inhaber. Die Wiedergabe von Marken, Produktnamen, Gebrauchsnamen, Handelsnamen, Warenbezeichnungen u.s.w. in diesem Werk berechtigt auch ohne besondere Kennzeichnung nicht zu der Annahme, dass solche Namen im Sinne der Warenzeichen- und Markenschutzgesetzgebung als frei zu betrachten wären und daher von jedermann benutzt werden dürften.

Bibliographic information published by the Deutsche Nationalbibliothek: The Deutsche Nationalbibliothek lists this publication in the Deutsche Nationalbibliografie; detailed bibliographic data are available in the Internet at http://dnb.d-nb.de.

Any brand names and product names mentioned in this book are subject to trademark, brand or patent protection and are trademarks or registered trademarks of their respective holders. The use of brand names, product names, common names, trade names, product descriptions etc. even without a particular marking in this work is in no way to be construed to mean that such names may be regarded as unrestricted in respect of trademark and brand protection legislation and could thus be used by anyone.

Coverbild / Cover image: www.ingimage.com

Verlag / Publisher:
LAP LAMBERT Academic Publishing
ist ein Imprint der / is a trademark of
OmniScriptum GmbH & Co. KG
Heinrich-Böcking-Str. 6-8, 66121 Saarbrücken, Deutschland / Germany
Email: info@lap-publishing.com

Herstellung: siehe letzte Seite /
Printed at: see last page
ISBN: 978-3-659-33407-8

ABSTRACT

THE REENTRY EXPERIENCES OF SEVEN FORMERLY INCARCERATED WOMEN

By Celeste R. Didlick-Davis

This qualitative study explored and promoted the understanding of factors that female formerly incarcerated citizen's experience and associate as significant challenges to successful family and community reintegration. This study focused on the issues that were identified in the literature; housing, employment, and supportive services as the keys to successful reentry. Unlike many previous reentry studies, this study focused exclusively on the experiences of females. Emergence of additional and/or alternative themes were identified including the importance of pre-release and post release programming and the significance of mentoring and other relationships upon successful reentry and reintegration. The experience of seven females and the barriers that impacted their reentry back into the southwestern Ohio community after their incarceration was the focus. The paper also presents limitations for this study and findings for future research and application.

THE REENTRY EXPERIENCES OF SEVEN FORMERLY INCARCERATED WOMEN

This work is dedicated to all the women who are returning home from incarceration and their families. Many do not ever understand how or why they got to such a dark place, more than two thirds of the women who are incarcerated have been victims of sexual, physical and emotional abuse. When a mother is incarcerated, so are her children, they are the innocent victims.

Table of Contents

List of Tables

Introduction

In America's cities former prisoners are everywhere. It is almost impossible to pick out ex-prisoners, after they are no longer required to wear prison uniforms and identification (Gonnerman, 2004). In fact, almost seven percent of the U.S. adult population, some 13 million people, has been convicted of a felony that results in incarceration (Gonnerman, 2004). Given such numbers, it is not surprising that more government dollars are spent on housing the offenders than on programs and rehabilitation (Gonnerman, 2004; Petersilia, 2003).

The concept of incarceration is both general and specific. There are characteristics that can be generalized regardless of physical location, age and gender of the incarcerated, type of crime committed, number of times incarcerated, and the type of facility in which the incarceration takes place. Incarceration can take place in a local or county jail, community-based correctional facility, halfway house, state or federal prison. Each incarceration experience is also unique because of the individuals involved. The experience of incarceration is influenced by numerous factors including the personalities of all of the stakeholders; which includes both prison personnel, other inmates, the family and friends who remain at home; and financial constraints. Current government statistics show us that women are the fastest growing inmate population in our jails and prisons today, with approximately 70% of the incarcerated females being mothers (Golden, 2005).

With such aforementioned considerations, this qualitative study explored the experiences of seven females reentering communities after a period of incarceration. Specifically, this research looked to uncover the barriers that exist upon release and those that continue to exist as well as the impact that these barriers might have had upon the individual's reentry. In addition, inquiry was made into the impact of the ex-offender's reentry on the family and the larger systems of neighborhoods and communities.

The theoretical framework supporting this research was family systems theory. The research design involved seven in-depth interviews with females who were previously incarcerated and were participating in the reentry process. All of the

1

participants in the study were incarcerated in Ohio. The structure of the interviews was designed to ascertain the participants" perceptions about reentry and the experiences of this group of individuals concerning reentry (Warren & Karner, 2005). The current study has implications on the possible best practices for reentry programs and contributes to the understanding of successful reentry and community reintegration. In particular, it is hoped, that the role of employment and economic self-sufficiency and their relationship to reentry and reintegration was explored.

The Problem

    Introduction.

New laws and sentencing guidelines enacted since the 1970s have resulted in a 300 percent increase in the American prison population between 1980 and 2000 (Reisig, Bales, Hay, & Wang, 2007). Each year more than 650,000 men and women return from prison (Mumola, 2000). Over the past generation, this country has embarked upon a social experiment in the criminal justice system that has had wide spread and often unknown implications (Visher & Travis, 2003). In fact, the per capita rate of imprisonment rose to 110 per 100,000 in 1973 to 470 per 100,000 in 2000 (Visher & Travis, 2003). Department of Justice studies of this population indicate that almost two-thirds of those individuals will return to prison within three years of release, many within the first few months. As a result, some researchers assert that inmate reentry into the community has only become a problem because of the criminal justice system's inability to keep pace in sheer volume and with the needs presented by offenders (Petersilia, 2003).

Reentry is the inevitable consequence of incarceration for many offenders (Travis & Visher, 2005). With very few exceptions everyone that is incarcerated eventually is released, on average 93% of those serving time in America will be released (Gonnerman, 2004). Reentry happens when incarceration ends; it is not a legal status, but a natural occurrence. Ex-offender reentry presents a new problem according to researchers for several reasons. First, more people are being released than ever before because more people are going to prison and because of overcrowding. Second, the needs of the incarcerated and the formerly incarcerated are more serious. Third, the corrections and rehabilitation systems are providing fewer rehabilitation programs. Fourth, new laws and public policies have systematically erected more legal barriers making reintegration more difficult. (Petersilia, 2003).

The consequences of incarceration have become more far-reaching and pervasive than ever before, not only affecting the offender and his or her family but also triggering a major shift in the family structure (Western, 2005). Factors associated with incarceration appear to impact overall life satisfaction of both individuals and families in the areas of low self-esteem, poor economic standing, reduced or absent supportive systems, the inability to find adequate employment and housing, and social stigma (Western, 2005).

Inmates being released now, as a whole will be less prepared for life on the outside because many states have decided to cut back on funding programs and services as well as the limitation of resources available to support reintegration after release. Collateral sanctions combined with the return of the formerly incarcerated into communities that are already struggling with high rates of unemployment and crime contribute to high rates of recidivism (Petersilia, 2003; and Visher & Travis, 2003). Some argue that lifelong stigma and barriers-declaring formerly incarcerated persons ineligible for certain governmental benefits- hinder successful reintegration (Petersilia, 2003; Visher & Travis, 2003). As a result, the outcomes associated with both inadequate transition planning and community supports present many barriers for ex-offenders and their reentry (Osher, 2007).

Historic and current issues: Female incarceration and reentry

Studies show that the result of an absence of a woman from the family is far more devastating than the absence of a man and that the family is more likely to deteriorate (Elsner, 2004). Incarceration rates generally have increased, but more importantly the number of women being incarcerated has also increased dramatically (Golden, 2005). In the 1960s and 1970s, a woman typically had to be arrested and have committed several separate crimes before she was sent to prison. Today with a change in sentencing laws, this is not the case (Golden, 2005 & Elsner, 2004). Unlike men, 70% of women incarcerated in state prisons were convicted of nonviolent crimes, (i.e. drugs, property crimes or petty financial offenses) (Elsner, 2004; personal communications Federal Judge Walter Rice, October 23, 2007). Approximately 70% of the females incarcerated are mothers. Two-thirds of the mothers incarcerated have children under the age of 18 (Golden, 2005).

One of the primary issues contributing to higher rates of incarcerated women was the enactment of the Comprehensive Crime Control Act (1984) during the Reagan Administration. America's war on drugs escalated during the Reagan administration with the Comprehensive Crime Control Act (1984). The bill, which focused on those involved in the street level of the drug trade, resulted in an explosion of women in jails and prisons. The sentencing components of both the Comprehensive Crime Control Act and the 1986 Anti-Drug Abuse Act with their mandatory minimum sentences had a significant negative impact on women (Golden, 2005).

In 2004 in an attempt to assist prisoner reentry, President Bush announced his Prisoner Re-Entry Initiative (PRI). According to PRI, reentry involves the use of programs targeted at promoting the effective reintegration of offenders back to communities upon release from prison and jail. In his 2004 State of the Union Address, President Bush reminded his audience that America is "the land of a second chance" (Travis & Visher, 2005). As an approach to providing a second chance, reentry programming, involves the use of a comprehensive case management approach which is intended to assist offenders in acquiring the life skills needed to succeed in the community and become law-abiding citizens (U.S. Department of Justice Office of Justice Programs [Reentry], 2004).

Through this program, returning offenders are linked to faith-based and community institutions that help ex-prisoners find work and avoid a relapse into a life of criminal activity. Currently there are 30 PRI grantees across the country that are providing mentoring, employment, and other transitional services to more than 5,789 participants (Bush, 2004). Despite some promising results with the Bush Prisoner Reentry Initiative (PRI), judges are currently sentencing female offenders at a higher rate than ever before (Elsner, 2004).

Demographics for the current female inmate populations indicate that two-thirds of the women in prison are minorities. About half of the current female population was youthful runaways, an untold number had serious drug problems and approximately 25% had attempted suicide, at least once prior to incarceration (Golden, 2005; Elsner, 2004).

Conservative estimates indicate that over 50% were victims of physical abuse and one-third victims of sexual abuse, 70% lacked a high school education and almost half had been unemployed prior to incarceration (Golden, 2005: Elsner, 2004). Twenty-three percent reported some type of mental illness, 20% were homeless prior to incarceration (Golden, 2005: Elsner, 2004). Many female inmates were from single-parent homes, had a family member who had been incarcerated and/or had been wards of the state at one time or another (Golden, 2005: Elsner, 2004).

The initial results of the PRI approach are promising (with high levels of employment and reduced recidivism rates), however, these programs do not reach all populations, geographic areas, or individuals who have not been incarcerated in prisons but have been housed in local jails (Reentry, 2004). Research shows that reentry does not just affect those incarcerated in state and federal correctional institutions (Osher, 2007). The outcomes associated with both inadequate transition planning and community support for the formerly incarcerated include public safety, a burden on services, hospitalization, suicides, domestic violence, homelessness, rearrest, and recidivism (Osher, 2007). On the other hand, economic stability is essential to achieving self-sufficiency and in most successful reentry programs includes employment, transitional housing and mentoring (Bush, 2004).

This study will contribute to reentry and community development by gaining insight from female formerly incarcerated citizens and the barriers they encountered in their reentry efforts to identify services and supports that might enhance the reentry experience of formerly incarcerated females and additional insight will be provided into the role of female reentry in family stabilization and well-being. Findings from this study can potentially be used to assist social service agencies, researchers, and policy makers to provide better services for formerly incarcerated females.

Literature Review

Women Behind Bars

The first American prison was authorized by the Pennsylvania state legislature in 1790 (O'Brien, 2001). This remodeled facility had previously been a jail and was opened as a penitentiary for children, women and men with separate facilities for the women and children (O'Brien, 2001). By 1860 the population was 57 white women and 24 black women, with the female population representing 18% of the total population (O'Brien, 2001). The first independent freestanding prison for women was built in Indiana in 1874 (O'Brien, 2001).

At the turn of the 20th century, the concept of a reformatory for women was promoted by Dorothea Dix (O'Brien, 2001). Reformatories for women also had indeterminate sentences and placed emphasis on being of sufficient moral character before being allowed to reenter society. The reformatories were the first instance of women being treated differently than women in the criminal system (O'Brien, 2001). Between 1900 and 1935, seventeen states opened women's correctional institutions. By the 1980s thirty-four women's institutions had been established (O'Brien, 2001). By the end of 1998, approximately one million women were under some form of correctional supervision, with over 150,000 being incarcerated in a correctional facility of some sort (O'Brien, 2001).

The criminal justice policies that have resulted in a dramatic increase in the female prison population have also generated much controversy (Golden, 2005; O'Brien, 2001; Osher, 2007; Travis & Waul, 2003). Many advocate more humane approaches than prison terms when dealing with problems of drugs and poverty and the type of crimes that most women commit (O'Brien, 2001). While not in agreement about whether or not prison or treatment or a combination of both is appropriate, there is an agreement that the significant negative impact on the family was not the intent of sentencing (O'Brien, 2001; Travis & Waul, 2003).

According to O'Brien (2001) prisons are not effective in helping women lead more productive, crime free lives after release, because many who leave prison are not better prepared to address the problems that got them locked up in the first place. However, some women do make the transition necessary and successfully return to the community and achieve personal satisfaction and social acceptability (Gonnerman, 2004; O'Brien, 2001).

Women offenders who are brought into the criminal justice system are disproportionately poor, undereducated, and people of color who have often been abused

6

and/or already marginalized and disenfranchised by the majority or mainstream society (Arditti & Few, 2006). The degree to which an individual was disenfranchised before incarceration can have a significant impact on reentry and reintegration after incarceration as well as the unique issues related to motherhood that female ex-offenders often encounter. Social support and family resource adequacy have been identified as two significant protective factors related to positive outcomes in reentry (Arditti & Few, 2006).

Despite the ever increasing population of women in prison, women in the United States are released from prison daily (O'Brien, 2001). Often they have little more than a few articles of clothing, some personal mementos, a little cash, and the well-wishes of a few buddies they are leaving behind (O'Brien, 2001). One of the primary differences between male and female offenders is that the male often has a home, a family or a significant other to return to as well as better opportunities to secure a legal, income-producing job that pays a living wage (O'Brien, 2001). In addition, a formerly incarcerated female might also have the challenge of regaining custody of her children and reconstructing the mother-child relationship (Travis & Waul, 2003; O'Brien, 2001). Contemporary feminist research also concludes that while men and women face some of the same challenges and barriers during and after incarceration, there are also some significant differences in both their incarceration and their reentry experience (Gonnerman, 2004; O'Brien, 2001; Travis & Waul, 2003). For example, women are often victims of abuse and rape while incarcerated, often having what they believe to be consensual relationships with guards and other employees (Elsner, 2004; T. Jones, personal communication, December 9, 2007). Women are often traumatized and subjected to unwanted advances as well as body searches and pat downs by male guards. Along these same lines, female prisoners are still plagued by the gender inequality and biases in prisons across the country that plague women generally (Elsner, 2004; Golden, 2005).

The issues of what is permissible concerning the male supervision and search of female prisoners has yet to come before the United State Supreme Court, as a result the individual states are free to establish policy in this area (Elsner, 2004). States also have different rules about when and under what circumstances a male employee may see a

7

female inmate naked. According to United States District Court Judge Cohn, in a July 2002 ruling, "Females being viewed by males is qualitatively different than males being viewed by females" (p. 135, Elsner, 2004).

Women often suffer from medical needs that go neglected or access to treatment is delayed by a lack of resources and high demand for these limited services (Petersilia, 2003). It is estimated that a higher percentage of the inmate populations either has AIDS or has tested HIV positive than in the United States generally. Prison inmates and releasees are generally less healthy-physically and mentally- than the population at large, whether a result of genetics or environmental factors such as risky lifestyles, and poor access to healthcare (Petersilia, 2003). Giving birth while incarcerated is another serious health issue for female prisoners. In many jurisdictions a pregnant inmate must give birth while shackled. As of 2001 only 15 states banned the restraint of a pregnant woman during labor and delivery (Elsner, 2004).

Because there are fewer women's prisons than men's prisons, women are more likely to be incarcerated farther away from home than men. All women in Ohio get processed through the Ohio Reformatory for Women, the main women's institution, located in Marysville Ohio. This prison, located in the western portion of the state, is also the only female institution that serves the mentally ill, maximum, and close security women offenders. The other intuitions are in Columbus and in northeast Ohio near Cleveland creating a considerable distance for many families to travel in order to visit an incarcerated female loved one.

Systems Theory: Women, Incarceration and the Family

Family systems theory, as it is commonly understood, emerged in the 1960s (Chibucos & Leite, 2005). A family is viewed as a system in which family members interact with one another, are interdependent to some degree, and exhibit connected, coherent behaviors surrounded by a boundary while also exhibiting certain shared and similar traits and characteristics (Chibucos & Leite, 2005). Each individual family member is also a subsystem within the family (Minuchin, 1985). From a systems perspective, the individual is conceptualized as interdependent, a contributing part of the system that also controls his or her behavior (Minuchin, 1985).

Family systems theory is based on several key assumptions:

8

1. All parts of the system are interconnected; the changes in one part of the family influence all other parts of the family (Minuchin, 1985; White & Klein, 2002).
2. Understanding of the family system is only possible by viewing the whole; which includes the assumption that one must consider the family in its entirety and that the family is greater than the sum of its parts (Minuchin, 1985; White & Klein, 2002).
3. A families" behavior affects its environment, and in turn the environment affects the family, i.e. resulting in some of the output of the system becoming input or feedback for the system (Minuchin, 1985; White & Klein, 2002).
4. Systems are heuristic, not real things or in other words, systems theory is a way of knowing more so that in reality it is a way of organizing a particular experience or set of experiences (Minuchin, 1985; White & Klein, 2002).

Conceptually, therefore a system is a unit that can be identified and that affects its environment (White & Klein, 2002). All systems have boundaries or borders, although some systems are more open than closed and some are more permeable than others (Minuchin, 1985; White & Klein, 2002). There are also rules of transformation or how the elements relate to one another and to the environment. All systems have access to resources but the variety of these resources can differ dramatically, representing very different options for families. Resources are obviously more than financial and include adaptability and how the system reacts to change (Minuchin, 1985; White & Klein, 2002). Systems also have levels, attempt to maintain balance or equilibrium and can include a host of subsystems (Minuchin, 1985; White & Klein, 2002).

Incarceration impacts the individual, the family, other subsystems, and the larger systems in which the individual or the family operated. At no time is the system more impacted than when a family member is arrested and jailed, or when the formerly incarcerated returns home (Bredehoft & Wallcheski, 2003; Mullis, Brailsford, & Mullis, 2005; Western, 2006). Because of the interconnectedness, the subsystems and the larger systems, make adjustments for change within the overall family system in order to function. These adjustments are survival necessities.

The family impacted by incarceration has often made adjustments during the incarceration period that have become comfortable. Often, family members are not willing to reconfigure the family again, especially if the adjustments seem to be working. When an incarcerated person was also the custodial parent, the changes for the child(ren) in the living arrangements can include changes in homes, rules, neighborhoods, and schools in addition to the psychological changes that accompany the incarceration of a family member (Boss, 1999; Chibucos & Leite, 2005; Mullis, Brailsford, & Mullis, 2005; Poehlmann, 2005).

To suggest that the incarceration of a female family member significantly impacts and alters the family system in addition to impacting community dynamics does not require a broad leap. As a result, individuals and families affect societies, the larger systems that they are a part of as well as their community (Bredehoft & Wallcheski, 2003). Often what happens within a family, especially how it is perceived by individual members as well as other systems has significance for family stabilization and community development (Bredehoft & Wallcheski, 2003; Mullis, Brailsford, & Mullis, 2005; Western, 2005).

Impact of Incarceration & Reentry

Depending on whom one asks- the purpose of incarceration changes. Some feel the purpose is strictly punitive; others feel that the purpose is both rehabilitation and correction while others view the purpose of incarceration as societal protection, and a deterrent to current and future criminals.   The ideology embraced or how the combinations of purposes are stressed, significantly impacts the incarceration experience (Herman, Osiris, & Villa; 2004).

Incarceration is also personalized experience that requires a certain mind set and certain socialization skills to survive no matter what the age, length of sentence, or place of incarceration. The rules governing the incarceration experience are often contradictory to the rules of a collective society. "I am not my brothers keeper and mind your own business" are more likely to be the rules that the incarcerated live by. The incarcerated are more likely to witness crime or criminal behavior on a daily basis, with the norm being

10

"see no evil, hear no evil, speak no evil" (V. Wright, personal communication, November 6, 2006). Often the setting of the incarceration has a significant impact on the attitude of the incarcerated person. The location of incarceration impacts whether any rehabilitation is attempted, the effectiveness of the rehabilitation attempts, and how long psychological impact of the incarceration lasts (whether positive or negative) (V. Bellman, personal communication, November 6, 2006).

In order to survive incarceration, it is necessary for the person to adapt both physically and psychologically. Unfortunately, it is often difficult for the formerly incarcerated to develop a more pro-social, engaged, community-connected mode of thinking and living without significant assistance by a host of resources and support. In fact, some have described incarceration as "a distortion of the state of belonging" (Herman, Osiris, & Villa; 2004). Herman, one of the co-authors of the materials used in "The Psychology of Incarceration" purports that being incarcerated distorts an individual"s normal state of belonging (Personal communication, May 3, 2006). Incarceration works to block opportunities for validation of social worth (Reentry, 2004).

Certain of the differences in the incarceration experience significantly impact the individuals" reentry needs and ability to obtain post release employment. Differences in incarceration experiences can include but are not limited to leisure time activity, job assignments, rule infraction histories, as well as what the individual was doing prior to incarceration. The type of family and friend contact is relevant to emotional and financial support while incarcerated as well as both financial and social support after incarceration (Reentry, 2004). Outside support is also a significant influence on the time management and the time displacement of the incarcerated person. Time displacement is defined as the time that one spends on a specific activity, i.e. incarceration, is time that is no longer available to be spent on another activity (J. Holmes, personal communication, March 20, 2007).

This increase in the movement from prison door to community doorstep comes at a time when traditional mechanisms for managing reentry have been significantly weakened. About one in five State prisoners leave prison with no post release supervision (Reentry, 2004). In many states, truth-in-sentencing statutes have curtailed the duration of post release oversight to 15 percent of the sentence imposed for violent offenders. Inadequately funded parole agencies in many jurisdictions have made parole more a legal status than a systematic process of reintegrating returning prisoners (Travis, 2000). Not all prisoners today, or historically, have been released under supervision (Gonnerman, 2004). Many who have been incarcerated are released directly into the community with no continuing obligation.

Parole boards have historically served a second important function—deciding whether a prisoner is "ready" to be released and supervising the development of a release "plan." Although imperfect, the system integrated the prerelease and post release functions of the relevant government agencies and provided a rationale for the offender's reentry. In the best of circumstances, the parole board would be able to say, „Harry Jones has made sufficient progress in his personal rehabilitation while in prison, and he has a network of family, neighborhood support, and work opportunities on the outside sufficient for us to determine he is ready to be released." The underpinnings of this approach have been severely criticized by research findings, public outcry, and political attacks from the left and right (Reentry, 2004). Rehabilitation programs were found by researchers to be ineffective; parole decisions were faulted as highly arbitrary; and parole supervision, even if intensive, was found not to reduce recidivism (Reentry, 2004). Finally, public pressure has undermined confidence in the parole system, particularly because of the highly visible, heinous crimes committed by some parolees who might otherwise have been in prison. In this environment, advocates of parole are having a hard time justifying its existence (Reentry, 2004).

Therefore, it is useful to note, based on the aforementioned discussion that reentry is a nearly universal experience for criminal defendants, not just returning prisoners (Gonnerman, 2004, Petersilia, 2003). Everyone- without exception-who is arrested and charged with a crime and then released [whether on bond, on probation, on parole or any other type of custody] transitions from a state of imprisonment (psychological and/or physically) to a state of liberty (Herman, Osiris, & Villa; 2004). Everyone who is released on bail, placed on probation after a period of pretrial detention, sentenced to weekend jail, or released to a drug treatment facility experiences a form of reentry.

When a person leaving prison or jail succeeds, the community succeeds. Ex-offender reentry is neither about ex-offenders nor the criminal justice system. Ex-offender reentry is about community. Therefore, it is essential for the community to be in the driver"s seat or at least a front seat navigator for reentry. In doing so, this may ensure the adequacy, appropriateness and availability of the human, social, political and financial resources so critical to the success of this effort (Reentry, 2004). Helping to restore the ex-offenders sense of belonging through mentoring, social support, and the provision of support services is a strategic role for community reentry organizations.

Method

Given the concerns previously mentioned, an exploratory, qualitative research design was used to obtain the experiences of seven females who were formerly incarcerated. The research design also involved using a non-probability convenience sample to obtain their perspectives on reentry, reintegration expectations and barriers they may have encountered in the community (Locke, Spirduso, & Silverman, 2000). The study was approved by the IRB of Miami University.

Participant Recruitment

Participants were recruited from an organization that is located in the southwestern part of Ohio by posting fliers on bulletin boards in a residential facility and a community agency that work with the formerly incarcerated. The residential facility has residential locations for formerly incarcerated females. One of the requirements for acceptance in the residential facility is that the client be transported to the facility directly from incarceration, usually by one of the facilities staff or volunteers. This residential program enables formerly incarcerated women to receive case management and supportive services in a safe environment that promotes stability of family. Considered a transitional home for women seeking supportive services after prison; this organization offers a six-month in-house program with two-year follow up on drug recovery and basic life skills. One of the facility residences can accommodate ten women at a time and the other residential unit, located in a public housing unit, can accommodate up to ten women and their children. The other agency is a community-based program which receives numerous referrals from sources throughout Montgomery County. These include the Department of Jobs and Family Services, the City of Dayton Mayor's office, and the Montgomery County Commissioners office. The community agency averages about 60 new referrals monthly with about 15-20% of the new referrals being women and maintains a client base of over 200 individuals. The community agency provides cognitive programming, referrals and a variety of assessment for the formerly incarcerated, as well as providing limited opportunities for paid and non-paid work experience.

Sample

The target population for the in-depth interviews was formerly incarcerated females. The participant sample consisted of seven females who have been incarcerated in Ohio and upon release from incarceration have remained in Ohio. The criteria for sample eligibility was that participants (1) must have a felony conviction, (2) must have been incarcerated in Ohio, (3) must have remained in Ohio after release from incarceration, and (4) must be female. Qualitative studies use a smaller number of participants than quantitative studies because of the volume of the data that must be analyzed as well as the potential goals of the study (Bailey, 2007; Creswell, 2003). The aim of qualitative research is to acquire an in-depth understanding of human behavior and the reasons that govern behavior (Warren & Karner, 2005). Consequently in a qualitative study, the need is for smaller but focused samples rather than large random samples (Bailey, 2007; Creswell. 2003; Warren & Karner, 2005). Along with meeting the eligibility requirements, written informed consent was obtained prior to the interview process.

Interview Procedures

In-depth interviews were conducted with seven female individuals who were formerly incarcerated. The primary goal of the interview was to ascertain the participant"s perspective about their reentry and reintegration experience. Using open-ended questions developed from the eight criminogenic domains used by the Ohio Department of Rehabilitation and Corrections. Insight was gained into the individual's reentry preparation and reentry experience resulting in an interpretation of the meaning of their reentry experience. (See Appendix A & B).

Interviews were tape recorded and field notes were made both during and immediately after the time of the interviews. Each of the tapes was then transcribed.

The transcriptions were then reviewed and proofread and compared with the field notes (Locke, Spirduso, & Silverman, 2000).

Results

This section presents the results of qualitative analysis. First, the description sample characteristics are discussed. Second, a phenomenological description of the major themes, which were revealed through the seven interviews with the formerly incarcerated women are discussed. This phenomenological description is derived from one central research question and eight associated central sub-questions which are based on the eight criminogenic domains. Interpretations of these results are included with the discussion in the following chapter.

Resulting Sample

The sample consisted of seven females residing in Montgomery County, Ohio, all of whom had been released from incarceration no longer than three years before the time of interview. One of the females, although having a felony conviction had not been incarcerated in the state penitentiary, but had been housed in a community-based corrections facility. Three of the seven females were living in a therapeutic community, (i.e. they were living in a behavior modification program). Four were living on their own, although two who were currently living in the community had also previously been residents of a behavior modification program immediately upon release from incarceration. Three of the participants had been members of a therapeutic community/behavior modification program during their incarceration prior to their release. Three of the seven participants were African American. The remaining four were Caucasian. Five of the seven were employed on some level at the time of the interview. Of the five that were employed, four had gotten their employment through relationships, referrals or friends of friends, some sort of networking. Only one of the seven individuals that I interviewed had gotten a job, just by walking into the door of an establishment and filling out a job application. (See Table 1).

All of the participants resided in an urban area with a population of fewer than 2,000,000 in southwestern Ohio at the time of the interview. The urban area served as the county seat as well as the center of the region in which it was located. The urban area is the fourth largest metropolitan area in Ohio. This urban area plays host to significant industrial, aerospace, and technological/engineering research activity and is known for the many technical innovations and inventions although it has been also adversely affected by the general state of the economy generally and the plight of the automotive, steel, paper, banking and information technology industries in particular.

Description of the Themes

The results of the data analyses are presented in terms of their relationships to the central research question and the eight criminogenic domain sub-questions, (i.e. what do formerly incarcerated females perceive as the barriers most significantly impacting their successful reentry and reintegration into the community and impacting family reunification). While the participants questions were centered on all eight of the criminogenic domains, as indicated by previous research, special attention was given to housing, employment and supportive services. The emerging themes that were identified included: The importance of supportive programming before release (while incarcerated) and immediately upon release, the importance of networking for employment, the importance of the role of stable housing in the absence of employment, and the substantial reliance on peer supportive services as a tool against relapse and recidivism. As a result of the aforementioned emerging themes, each of these themes will be discussed individually.

Therefore the results of this data analyses are presented in terms of their relationship to the research questions that guided this study. This methodology will provide a phenomenological picture of the reentry and reintegration experiences of formerly incarcerated females immediately after their release from incarceration in terms of their challenges and the barriers they face.

Sub-question one.

Since your release and reentry into the Community, what has your experience been with employment opportunities? For the Ohio Department of Rehabilitation and Corrections, this domain deals with the role of work in the offender's life. Assessment includes employment history, if any; positive and negative aspects of the work history (such as job performance, absenteeism, unstable work record, having been fired, inability to earn sufficient salary to live on, having difficulty with co-workers and/or superiors), and vocational skills. The purpose of this question was to determine how prepared the participants were for employment upon their release from incarceration, what their employment status had been prior to incarceration, what their level of participation was in employment readiness programs during incarceration and what had been their experiences seeking employment since their release.

Participant #1 shared here employment history and experience: "I worked odd jobs before I was incarcerated but now I am employed at uniform company". She reported that she got her job "through someone that she knew who worked there". (Actually several of the ladies who are living in the residential facility for formerly incarcerated women work at the same company.) When asked how are people getting jobs today? Her response "Relationships or someone they know".

Participant #2 reported her employment experience

I consider myself to be blessed compared to some people. I connected with a woman at the mall and I was offered a job. She did not know my situation. She suspected that something was odd and I did confess to her the first day that I was hired. I ended up working for a lot less. It was a $7.00 an hour position where I was paid as a subcontractor, so I filed my own taxes. I was grateful to have a job.

How did you meet this woman?

She had the aqua massage at the Dayton Mall and I had just gotten out of prison and was at the Mall with my daughter. I said I don"t know what it is, but I want one. I rode the aqua massage and we just connected. When I got off, my daughter told her that I was a massage therapist but I cannot practice because of my felony. She thought it would be good working with people selling her product. She offered me the job. Then I got laid off. I worked for her for close to a year and she went through a divorce and sold the business. Then I went on welfare, and worked as a volunteer at an agency that works with the ex-offenders as part of my welfare assignment. I did that for another year until I recently became a paid employee part-time. It"s been hard because I have a family to keep. The time for me to find a job is now. Someone helped me because they knew the person at the company where I work at now.

So, you got your job through a connection? Participant # 2 "Yes".

Participant #3 reports that prior to her incarceration she was also unemployed "Unemployed, but I had my own other stuff".

Participant #5 shared her employment experience:

"I was released in September 2001. At first it was not a problem because I came out and went back to a previous employer. It was not until he decided to close his doors in 2006 that I found how hard it was for a felon to obtain employment". What kind of work have you been looking for?

> I tried to go into my field, business information systems, I know that I am qualified for NCR, Reynolds & Reynolds, Lexus Nexus, City of Dayton, and the County [Montgomery], none of them would hire me. I am currently working as a bartender in a club, after a long period of unemployment, a friend of mine's uncle owns the place.

Based on the qualitative data obtained from the client's responses to Sub-question one, the themes that emerged were the importance of networking (in order to gain any type of employment) and the importance of participating in programming and supportive services not directly related to employment. The criterion used for establishing emergent themes was a response by two or more participants, regardless of which sub-question was being answered. Recognition of the commonalities of the participant's statements concerning the importance of and the heavy reliance on networking through associations, social interactions and community functioning combined with either supportive family members and/or a supportive living environment was a significant thread throughout sub-question one. Also apparent in the literature is that women offenders brought into the criminal justice system are disproportionately poor, undereducated, and people of color that have often been already marginalized and disenfranchised by the majority or mainstream society (Arditti & Few, 2006). The degree to which an individual was disenfranchised before incarceration had a significant impact on the type and the amount of supportive services, wrap around services and programming needs that an individual had, especially an incarcerated or formerly incarcerated female.

Sub-question two.

What has been your experience since your release from incarceration with identifying educational opportunities? For the Ohio Department of Rehabilitation and Corrections, this domain is educational deficiencies (including intelligence, learning disabilities). Programming in this domain deals with the role of education in the offender"s life including any deficiencies in education as well as on participation and achievement in academic or vocational education programs, completion of an apprenticeship, career training in a field suitable for post-release employment, and other programs designed to assist offenders in looking for, applying for, and retaining a job.

The purpose of this question was to determine how prepared the participants were to identify educational opportunities upon their release from incarceration, to determine whether identifying educational opportunities was even a priority or a reality for the women upon their release from incarceration and to determine what their experiences were as they related to education.

The participants" experiences as well as their attitudes and educational levels concerning education and identifying opportunities were very diverse with some of the women still needing to obtain their GEDs and others having more than one college degree even before incarceration.

In response to the question Participant # 2 said "Try to get my GED I want to get into social work and try to be a counselor or case-worker."

Participant #3"s response: "I have three degrees already", (prior to being incarcerated). May I ask what your degrees are in? "Microcomputers, Data Processing, Computer Software Engineering and Business Administration". At least two of the women were currently pursuing their educations and several more expressed an interest in eventually pursuing additional education.

One of the women (#1) had experienced some challenges with going back to school because of her felony status but she was eventually able to enroll in school and receive financial assistance. "I was not able to get back into school until two years later because of some government criteria pertaining to felons". So, you have problems with the felony financial aid? "Yes." Did something change? "There is a time limit from the time you actually commit the offense and I think it's a three year or five year time limit. I was convicted in 1998 and I could not go back to school until 2003 because that's when it would be listed." Has financial aid been difficult? What is going on with the school?

School is fine. Now, it is more or less that I got discouraged. Why am I going to school if I cannot find a job? Why does the government give me money to get an associate or bachelor in business and I cannot use it. That's like giving a felon a medical degree and he cannot use it. It makes no sense.

Participant # 4 responded similarly when asked what has been your experience since your release from incarceration with identifying educational opportunities. "Not a problem. (But I already had 2 degree's prior to incarceration) Which I have not used since my release".

Another of the women (Participant #5) indicated that, while she had been interested in attending school and had even applied to some schools while she was still incarcerated, she found she really did not have the time to pursue additional education at this time because of the of the number of hours she needed to work in order to support herself.

> When I was in Tapestry, I had filled out all the federal-aid forms to make sure that I was good when I got out and I could go straight back. It didn't quite happen like that. I had to rearrange my goals because working was more important at that time. I needed the money. The schedule at my job was hectic. I worked days and nights, so education fell on the back burner.

While education is and still continues to be an area of importance for reentering citizens, it is often overshadowed by the real and pressing need to find employment and achieve economic self-sufficiency, regardless of the educational level or lack of education of the individual.

Sub-question three.

Since your release from incarceration and reentry into the Community, what has been your experience concerning your family relationships (including marital relations, if applicable)? For the Ohio Department of Rehabilitation and Corrections, this domain is concerned with the role with an offender's family relationships, including relationships with parents and siblings, absence of parents, history of family abuse and/or criminality, marital history, dependents, parenting skills, and involvement in child abuse. The rationale behind this question was that family support or the lack of it is often a primary indicator of the likelihood of recidivism and reentry success.

The vast majority of returning inmates on supervision are released to a family member. Many on supervision who are required by parole to enter a halfway house or transitional living situation do so because of the lack of appropriate housing with family or a negative family situation. While the numbers of beds in transitional living and behavior modification facilities are extremely limited, participation in these types of facilities has

20

been shown to positively impact recidivism outcomes. For many strained family relationships is often a primary contributor to relapse and recidivism. Family relationships are often one of the reasons formerly incarcerated cite as contributing to the need for supportive programming and additional community functioning resources, while others cite their family relationships as being an important element to their successful reentry experience.

Participant # 1 "My mom and youngest daughter support me. My oldest daughter has disowned me. My husband and I cannot get along anymore (he is using) and we are calling it quits".

Participant # 2 "My marriage did not work".

Participant #3 reported

My husband didn't like me or talk to me for the whole three years that I was gone. I was in prison for two, but really gone for a year prior to that. I was quite sure what was going to happen with that when I got out, but we reunited and I went back to my house with my husband and my children.
We have a better relationship now than we ever had. We both grew up while I was gone. My parents and I really have a great trusting relationship. I was real honest with them while I was gone. They came to visit me. They would call me for advice or to help them do things. I call them and talk to my sister everyday.

Participant #5 also talked about having difficult times mending her family relationships.

It has been rough and continues to be. I am not on speaking terms with my son aside from arguments and emails. My daughter has been in and out of the hospital with suicidal tendencies in cutting herself. She is incredibility angry and she is presently out of the house because she is verbally abusive and very angry.

Participant #4 was forced to move in with her daughter upon her release and when she lost her employment she had to move back in with her daughter and while the relationship is positive, having to live with her daughter is also a stressor.

Family relationships continue to be a significant factor for females returning from incarceration. While the impact of their relationships varies significantly; they range from supportive, to non-existent, to conflictual. Yet, the family remains important, even for those whose relationships are strained or minimal. Many of these females returning to

21

the community from incarceration could not do so without financial, emotional, and material support. For many of these ladies who do not have access to transitional living settings, or behavior modification programs, living with family members or friends, is not an option, although some are willing to provide some sort of support, even if only moral. For many retuning from incarceration, regaining, restoring or building healthy family relationships is a goal.

Sub-question four.

What has been your experience since your release from incarceration with associations and social interactions? For the Ohio Department of Rehabilitation and Corrections, this domain focuses on the characteristics and qualities of the offender's interactions with others, particularly the offender's peer group(s). Anti-social associates and interaction patterns are of special interest to the Ohio Department of Rehabilitation and Corrections, but some of the responses of the participants in the current study support the fact that positive associations and social interactions are equally if not more important than the absence of negative associations and social interactions.

Participant #5 reported "I don't have friends so I have peace of mind". Another participant (#4) responded that it was not the negative associations but the lack of positive associations that was troublesome for her. For example she reported

> I did not do very much of anything with my spare time. It has been depressing and I relapsed. I started drinking. My fiancé is still incarcerated, so I really don't do a whole lot. Sit at home on the weekends. It's gotten better now and I am starting do some things.

One participant (# 6) indicated that one of the reasons that she moved to a new location had to do staying near positive associates and away from past bad associations.

> There are a couple of people that I know; most of them are mainly the ones that graduated from the Monday Program. I have stayed in contact with them with me being new to the area. They are helping me to get around, guide me and tell me where things are. I have met some people at the NA meetings that I talk to.

Many of the participants interviewed talk about the importance of their support networks, whether they cite peer support groups such as AA or NA, alumni gatherings of the formerly incarcerated (a group that is unique to participants in the Tapestry Program at the Ohio Reformatory for Women), and support derived from the participation in religious based services or housing alternatives. Many indicated that they were required to make and develop new associations and social interactions and only a few individuals indicated that they did not engage in any interactions outside their home or work environment. Participant # 7 responded "I really do not associate with too many people at all; I guess coworkers and AA members. I don't talk to many people". Another participant (#2) reported

> I don't talk to anyone that I used to talk to before. My new friends are those that I mainly meet at work...it is a family-owned business. There is a girl there who is ten years younger than me and another one that is maybe five years younger. I think of them as working associates and not really friends. I don't really go out because of money and that kind of thing. I've never been the type of person that had a whole bunch of friends. I really had maybe two before I went to prison, that I could call or whatever.

Sub-question five.

What has been your experience since your release from incarceration with substance abuse? For the Ohio Department of Rehabilitation and Corrections, this domain is concerned with an offender's problems, if any, with alcohol abuse, drug abuse, and with any prior treatment programs. It includes details concerning the substance abuse, the extent to which alcohol or other drugs interfered with the offender's pro-social experiences (such as marital/family relations, employment, and social situations), and information about prior substance abuse treatment programming. One participant (#1) reported "My one friend from tapestry who I hung out with when I first got out, she relapsed and went back to prison, but there are still several girls that I still talk to from tapestry and I consider them friends". While some of the participants have reported no experience with any substances since their release, others have either relapsed or engaged in the use of alcohol and other drugs on some recreational level, whether or not they identified themselves as having a substance abuse pre-incarceration problem or not. For example when asked about her alcohol use, one participant (#6) replied

> I'm choosing not be an all or nothing person. I don't think it has to be that way. I am fifty years old and if I want to have a beer now and then or go out and have a glass of wine, I going to. I abhor my addictive tendencies and things that I can use as a crutch. Some things have changed. I pray for release of that.

23

Another participant (#2) indicated that her employment needs forced her into a less than desirable environment, one that included alcohol and possible drug use.

> When I came home, I changed the people, places and things that I associated with, so the people that I associated with ten years ago, I no longer associated with which. That brings me back to the job situation. I am forced to put myself back into an environment that I don't want to be in, but I have to in order to get the money.

For those participants who admitted to use, some of the reasons relating to use included stress and frustration as well as a belief that some use was acceptable, often even while acknowledging that it could be problematic. Others indicated that being around "their drug of choice" often created feelings of anger and frustration or relief depending on the circumstances and that at times their choice to engage in high risk behavior was not always well thought out.

Sub-question six.

Since your release from incarceration and reentry into the Community, what has been your experience with community functioning? For the Ohio Department of Rehabilitation and Corrections, this domain considers the offender's capability for functioning adequately in the community. The domain covers a wide range of community living skills that reflect stability: well-maintained place of residence, health needs, hygiene and nutrition, financial management skills, appropriate leisure time activities, and awareness of available social assistance programs. While still incarcerated in a traditional institutional setting, much of the programming available for inmates in this area can only have a limited impact at best. Programming in this domain should focus on knowledge and skill acquisition in the specific areas identified as deficient. "Life skills" programs and release preparation programming also contribute to addressing needs in this area, the very nature of the inmate"s living environment, the institutionalization of the inmate, if you will, limits the effectiveness of much of the programming in this area, especially where it involved female inmates. Much of the decision-making is taken away from the incarcerated and definitely the need to multi-task (be responsible for oneself and one"s children) is non-existent while incarcerated for many inmates unless they are housed in behavior modification/therapeutic housing units. For example, one participant (#4) shared "because I came from a place where I was in a crack house and there was

24

no structure whatsoever... the MonDay has taught me a lot about right living and myself". While another (#6) emphasized the importance of stability and learning "how not to fall back into old ways that will put you back into old habits and get you into the same situation just a new time".

Sub-question seven.

What has been your experience since your release from incarceration with personal and emotional orientation (this would include your behavior, how you think, and problem-solving skills)? For the Ohio Department of Rehabilitation and Corrections, this domain covers a multi-faceted and wide range of personal and emotional need factors that have been shown to be predictive of criminal and recidivistic behavior. This dimension includes needs that fall into three major categories: Cognitive defects, which include problem-solving, inter-personal relationship skills, inability to understand the feelings of others, and narrow, rigid thinking; Behavioral problems, including behaviors likely to result in negative consequences, such as impulsivity, risk-taking, aggression, anger, frustration tolerance and gambling; Personal Characteristics, which may increase the likelihood that the offender will be involved in criminal behavior (e.g., personality dispositions, behavioral preferences [including inappropriate sexual attitudes and/or risky behaviors], and mental status characteristics). While ODRC addresses some of the needs in this domain through the use of Mental Health Services, for the remainder of the inmates, the programming in this area focuses on addressing cognitive and behavioral needs in the areas of problem-solving, coping with stress, anger management, cognitive restructuring, and impulsive decision-makings or risk-taking behavior.

One participant (#1) indicated that the transition from incarceration to freedom has not been smooth.

> I get lonely, I get depressed and I get on my pity pot. Sometimes I try to loose myself in my work, which is easy to do because there is always a lot to do. It's an escape thing. I'm starting counseling. I decided to put myself back into that. Because I am on Prozac, I needed to get medical coverage. I went into Crisis Care and was referred to East Way. I took advantage of all the help that I could get. I went into a women's trauma group dealing with some of the abusive relationships. The whole prison experience is traumatic.

Another participant (#4) reported "I am not a religious person. I believe in God and I know right from wrong. I think about my choices, whereas before [incarceration] I did not care".

A third participant (#6) shared her experience and outlook:

One thing that I think is very stressful when you come home is being in a relationship. It took me until last week to realize how stressful it is to be in a relationship. If you have just come home, you should not be in a relationship unless you know that you are mentally ready for that. You are torn between trying to find a job and not doing enough. You have the guilt that you can't help. Everything is not about money and it shouldn't be. It also looks good on resumes. It makes you feel good at the end of the day. You think about how you made someone else's day by doing something and not wanting something in return. It helps a lot in our situation because it shows that we are trying to change or do something different.

Sub-question eight.

Since your release from incarceration and reentry into the Community, what has been your experience with attitude, your own attitude and the attitudes of others you encounter (those you encounter regularly and also infrequent or incidental encounters)? For the Ohio Department of Rehabilitation and Corrections, this domain considers the characteristics and extent of the offender's pro-social and anti-social attitudes. It is concerned with favorable attitudes toward crime and violence and minimization of the impacts of criminal behavior and disregard for convention, the justice system, and the rights of others, developing and fostering non-criminal thinking, emphasis on victim awareness and empathy, and the development of pro-social values.

This question was often misunderstood by participants, for instance one participant (#6) replied:

My attitude ~ swings with my moods, [as far as my attitude towards] others ~ it varies. In general, people's attitudes are negative and hateful. Towards me ~ those who know me are friendly; others are leery and a few just plain out try to avoid me. In meeting someone for the first time who does not know my background, they are nice, but I find that I am the leery, stand-offish one.

Another participant (#7) responded, "My attitude is that I don't take nothing for granted, I have to remain humble and I know that no one owes me nothing".

Participant #5 related when asked What about your experience with your attitude, your attitude with others that you encounter regularly?

I have more appreciation than I ever had for the small things in life. I enjoy coming to work, even though I want to tear my hair out most days when I am here. I find what I do every rewarding. It helps me find a purpose to heal from the whole prison experience.

While the Ohio Department of Rehabilitation and Corrections" intent was to focus on attitude towards criminal behavior, the respondents seemed to believe that the focus of the question was about them personally more so than about criminal thinking. I allowed the participants to provide the responses as they interpreted the question because it also reflected the disconnect that often exists between the Ohio Department of Rehabilitation and Corrections language and what the participants were thinking. Also most, if not all of the participants, believed that criminal thinking was something in their past and no longer an area for concern.

Emerging Themes

Four primary themes emerged from the interviews with the participants. While in many respects these themes had been eluded to in the literature review and previous research, these four emerging themes are also unique and not entirely identical to the previous research. Again, the criterion for determining emerging themes was that at least two participant responses. The first theme is the importance of supportive programming either before the inmate is released or (while incarcerated) and immediately upon release. Many of the problems that plagued the participants did not and could not be addressed without participating in programming that was specifically designed to address the underlying root causes for the individual's dysfunctional or criminal behavior. More often than not the behavior began long before the arrest that resulted in imprisonment.

Most of the women that I interviewed indicated that they could not have made it without some sort of support, often even just a place to go to help pass the time or a place that was supposed to help them get back on their feet. Many reported that they learned some things about themselves in the programs that they participated in while incarcerated. They indicated that groups like anger management, domestic violence classes and substance abuse awareness helped them to begin to take a look at their situations. While the motives for enrolling in these programs were often not strictly for self-improvement, many related that the longer that they participated in these programs, the more they began to see themselves grow.

Several of the women had participated in a residential therapeutic program called Tapestry and most indicated that participating in this program made a significant difference in their reentry experience. Many who had not participated in any significant program while incarcerated indicated that, especially in an economy and community where unemployment was already high, that if they had not had the luxury of being in a residential program they would have felt more pressures. Many of the women have formed informal and others have formed more formal support groups comprised of other formerly incarcerated and/or recovering women. Some have formed informal groups by the nature of their living arrangements, while others have more formal groups that meet regularly. For some, it is not so much that they attend these meetings every month but that they know where to find a gathering, if they need it and for others, the monthly meetings are a major part of the reentry support. Yet another subset keeps in contact through the internet.

One of the major differences between those who participated in residential programming before release from incarceration and those who participated after is the diversity of their experiences and the fact that some of their experiences during their incarceration are similar creating another unique bond. For example, all of the women who participated in the Tapestry program at the Ohio Reformatory for Women shared a similar experience, regardless of when they were incarcerated or even whether they were incarcerated at approximately the same time. The Tapestry program encourages the women to maintain contact with the program staff and current residents, but also to attend "alumni" meetings held in various regions monthly as well as several gatherings annually that are held throughout the state. Whether the women chose to take advantage of this support network it is always there.

For the women who participate in residential programs after release from incarceration, by participating in the programs, they automatically had stable housing, support, and employment or career counseling assistance.

Participant #4 reports on her life before incarceration Interviewer's question [IQ]: What did you do before you were incarcerated? "Worked odd jobs".

IQ: What kind of job would you like to have, if you could have a certain job? "I haven't thought about it". Do you have any goals for education? "I don't know". Participant #4 lives in a supportive residential program where with the assistance of the program staff she can get career development assistance as well as some leads to employment, more importantly, she will receive some sort of case management services, can you imagine this person living having been released with no stable housing, because she was not on probation or parole and no person or agency being charged with the responsibility to help her get her life back on track? Many in residential settings benefit from a case management system as well as having structure imposed on their lives, which worked as a step down system from the structured institutional life. Especially for those women who had not had any extensive programming while incarcerated, this step down and support is often invaluable. In addition to having a case manager, there are also usually several job leads already in existence because of the employment situations of other residents. For example, several of the residents work at the same facilities. This is also true of the men's halfway house and therapeutic treatment facilities in the area.

The second theme to emerge was the importance of networking for employment. In many respects this theme, the importance of networking to secure employment, is not really different for the formerly incarcerated and those who have not been formerly incarcerated. I recently participated in the National Training for Global Career Development Facilitators and statistics shared during the course of this 135 hour training by the Instructor Carol A. Wargo indicate that most people find employment through networking and relationships (personal communication, April 23, 2009). In today's job market, despite the use of the internet, the classifieds, and walking in and filling out applications, the majority of the workforce gets employment "not just on what you know but also who you know" (C. Wargo, personal communication, April 23, 2009). Also important to mention is that in an especially tight economy, with increasing layoffs of non-felons, high unemployment, and an increased immigrant population, combined with the shift away from capital and labor intensive occupations, the demand for unskilled labor is declining. While not all of the female formerly incarcerated in the labor force are without skills, for many without personal relationships, or introductions, the majority of the jobs that they are most likely to qualify for are unskilled or clerical.

The third theme to emerge is the importance of stable housing especially in the absence of employment. While many formerly incarcerated are released to family members" homes or to the homes of close friends, many times due to parole rules, the formerly incarcerated cannot return to the place they lived before incarceration. The reasons vary. Sometimes, the most stable home or place to return after incarceration is not available because of someone else in the home's criminal record. At other times, the decision to let someone stay is because they had nowhere else they could return, but the situation is not stable because "I really want you to move somewhere else as soon as possible, like yesterday" (D. Jemison, personal communication, May 17, 2007). Many times, the place where the formerly incarcerated is staying is actually in someone's den or on the living room couch, increasing the instability of the placement. The instability of the placement also intensifies the need for employment and a strong support system after release and increases the likelihood of relapse and relapse triggers.

The fourth and final emerging theme that will be discussed the substantial reliance on peer supportive services as a tool against relapse and recidivism. Participant #1 reports that

> My husband didn't like me or talk to me for the whole three years that I was gone. I was in prison for two, but really gone for a year prior to that. I was quite sure what was going to happen with that when I got out, but we reunited and I went back to my house with my husband and my children.

So when she needs to talk she must find other outlets, for that she uses her Tapestry sisters, either through meetings and alumni gathers, the internet or telephone.

Participant #2 reported that before she became involved with a community organization and task force that engages in reentry activities and where she has been reconnected to other formerly incarcerated persons, despite having employment she was in a constant depressed state and relapse mode.

30

It has been depressing and I relapsed. I started drinking. I am starting to use some of the tools that are available to me. I get lonely, I get depressed and I get on my pity pot. Sometimes I try to loose myself in my work, which is easy to do because there is always a lot to do. It's an escape thing. I'm starting counseling. I decided to put myself back into that. Because I am on Prozac, I needed to get medical coverage. I went into Crisis Care and was referred to East Way. I took advantage of all the help that I could get. I went into a women's trauma group dealing with some of the abusive relationships. The whole prison experience is traumatic. Some things have changed. I pray for release of that. At first, I was totally lost. The fact that I started to volunteer for PowerNet [PowerNet of Dayton is a community organization that specializes in working with the formerly incarcerated, it is a community based, non-residential program] that I started to learn about resources for myself as well as for others. I have finally begun to reach out more and I also have a couple of positive relationships with a couple of the women that I was incarcerated with.

Participant #7 reports on the importance of positive peer support as well as stable housing to her current successful reentry: she related her reentry experience of five years ago

About five years ago. I was on disability, so a job was no big thing to me. I smoked up my checks, went back to the streets, caught another assault charge and went back to prison for more time. Two things that contributed most to my not making it when I came home five years ago were my ex- boyfriend and drugs.

When you left, did you have a place to go? "No. I went back to him". You were receiving disability before you were incarcerated this time? "Yes". How did you spend your time before? "With him". This obvious lack of a positive peer support system, supportive programming and stable housing speak volumes.

Discussion

Interpretation and discussion of the qualitative results are included in this chapter. The literature, which helps to better explain and enhance understanding of the results are compared with the conclusions drawn in this study. Research implications from the present study will be discussed. Finally, improvement for this study and its limitations will be presented.

31

Literature Based Interpretation of Qualitative Results

Bailey (2007) acknowledges that the goal of qualitative interpretation is what can be explained beyond the limits of understanding or interpretation with the degree of certainty usually associated with analysis. As such, the researcher attempts to answer the importance of the research and the application of the research. Therefore, the most significant findings provide important insights into the quality of life of formerly incarcerated females and their families and the larger systems to which they return.

The foundation of Family Systems Theory is that the progress or well-being of the individual significantly impacts the larger systems of family and community. Consequently, when the formerly incarcerated female is released and attempts to return to her family and community, any barriers that she faces also affect her family and community reintegration. While family support is important, equally if not more important is the transformation and supportive programming of the individual. The likelihood for positive reentry and community reintegration outcomes increases when the formerly incarcerated have been able to address through programming and reentry planning most or all of these domains.

While previous research has shown for the most part prisons are not as effective *without interventions or programming* in helping women who need it most lead more productive, crime free lives after release, because many who leave prison have not participated in the types of programming that is designed to address the problems that got them locked up in the first place (O'Brien, 2001). There are numerous reasons contributing to this phenomenon including the length of sentencing, the length of the waiting list for certain types of programming, the financial strains of the prison system, as well as the unpopularity or unattractiveness of many of these residential programs. Especially at the beginning of an inmate's sentence, there is often a distain for what seems to be additional rules (of residential programs) within an already very structured environment. There is also the attractiveness of programs such as education, anger management, and substance abuse that do not require participation in a residential program. While some of the women who are incarcerated came with solid employment histories and strong job skills, many did not. As with any group of individuals or any bell curve, some will not need to help and some will not want the help representing the outliers of the prison population, while the majority need some assistance, although the level if assistance varies greatly. Research indicates some women do make the transition necessary for successful return to the community and achieve personal satisfaction and social acceptability (Gonnerman, 2004; O'Brien, 2001) with minimal assistance and little or no programming while incarcerated. While this qualitative project cannot be generalized because of the nature of the study, in actuality when looking at the topic of employment, the responses from the participants speak volumes; the majority of formerly incarcerated women acquire their employment opportunities as a result of networking and referrals. Actually this is not so much different than job seekers generally, in the current workforce (C. Wargo, personal interview, March 9, 2009). The majority of job seekers who actually obtain employment do so through some sort of networking. Networking, for the purposes of this writing is being defined as information and referral sharing and/or personal recommendations about job opportunities and assistance with getting past the gatekeepers (C. Wargo, March 9, 2009).

Implications

This descriptive qualitative study provided further insights into formerly incarcerated females" experiences and the complexity of the reentry experience, including the importance of programming and supportive services both before and after release from incarceration. The participants of this study suggest that behavior modification programming whether before or after release from incarceration is a significant factor in successful reentry programming. Findings from the participants suggest that positive peer support, such as that used in traditional twelve step programs are also important to successful; reintegration for formerly incarcerated females.

Additionally, this study provided useful information in a variety of ways. First, research from these participants present implications for family life education, corrections and reentry programming. Second, these findings also reveal possible implications related to policy. Lastly, there are implications for future research which will assist social service agencies and pre- and post- release and reentry programming. Thus, the implications for future research will also serve to validate and enhance existing findings while giving additional rise to additional areas for services and programming development.

Family Life Education, Corrections and Reentry Programming

Family Life Education can perhaps use the qualitative findings that evolved from this study to better assist families of the formerly incarcerated. In order to provide better support for their formerly incarcerated loved one as well as to better understand the importance of networking, supportive services, and peer support groups. Family life education may wish to develop a workshop for the families of the formerly incarcerated which disseminates information that is especially relevant for families impacted by incarceration. For example, many families impacted by incarceration are information about how to obtain a variety of services to assist with their newly created kinship care situations such as insurance and healthcare, legal assistance with custody and child support and counseling. Also of importance are family support groups to help the family better handles many of the issues related to having an incarcerated family member. In addition Family Life Educators as well as Corrections and Reentry personnel could choose to facilitate the creation of networking opportunities and peer support groups for both the individuals and families impacted by incarceration. Case managers might also expand the services that they provide to individuals and families impacted by incarceration to include networking and peer support opportunities.

Policy and Research Implications

With the increase in incarcerated females as well as the changes upon the family structure and dynamics that accompany incarceration, it becomes even more important that policy makers and others reconsider the issues of collateral sanctions and rehabilitation certificates. In addition, information technology and the fact that no record is ever really sealed or expunged, also warrant a policy review. Both of these issues have significant impact on both the formerly incarcerated individual's and the family's economic self-sufficiency and viability. While many who are released from incarceration are eligible for some government assistance immediately upon release, often this eligibility period is not long enough. Also many of the jobs that are considered to be in high demand are in industries that traditionally do not hire the formerly incarcerated, (i.e. the healthcare industry). There are also numerous prohibitions concerning housing, licensing, travel, and receipt of certain kinds of federal assistance that impede the formerly incarcerated and their families. With limited or no opportunities to earn certificates of rehabilitation and a lack of a national concerning rehabilitation certificates, many of the formerly incarcerated are forever barred from a number of opportunities. Combining the aforementioned items with the lower wages that females are already paid as well as the higher percentage of women that are custodial parents, results in long-term crises for families of formerly incarcerated females.

Potential policies regarding the unexpected burden and numerous stressors that female parental incarceration creates on the family structure must also be addressed by practitioners and policy makers. Not all children impacted by incarceration are involved in formal placement relationships, nor do all of these children benefit from services such as mentoring and supportive services. Children have long been called the unintended victims of parental incarceration and consideration to this vulnerable group of should be acknowledged.

Further research is necessary to fully explore the long term implications of female incarceration on both the individual and the family. While much research has been conducted concerning incarceration, in general, only recently has research on female incarceration become more prevalent. As such, continued research is necessary concerning female incarceration and reintegration into the community.

Limitations

While using a qualitative research design provides useful information about female barriers to successful reentry and reintegration, limitations exist in the current study. The limitations of this present study along with suggestions for areas of improvement will be discussed in this section. The following limitations should be considered:

Although appropriate for qualitative studies, the sample size and procedures for participant selection do not support generalization to a larger population, (Locke, Spirduso & Silverman, 2000). Generating interest and participation in the study through fliers might have also recruited individuals who were more motivated and possibly more likely to have some sort of support mechanisms in place. In addition, many of the individuals who were experiencing more challenges to successful reentry and reintegration were less likely to visit the organizations where the fliers were posted.

Along these same lines, the study was limited to participants in and around a small major city in Southwestern Ohio. A few of the participants that were also residents in the behavior modification program, although willing to participate in the study, did not have any real experience with reentry because they had just been released and were still in the program's restricted movement phase. Another group of interested respondents, who lived in the community, were unable to be interviewed for a number of reasons including scheduling, missed appointments, a lack of follow through and communication breakdown. Second, mortality also occurred. Some of the participants who originally indicated a willingness to participate in the study dropped out due to losing interest, moving out of the area or being released from programs. Also it was not feasible to revisit the residential facility.

Lastly, having worked with some of the individuals in a professional capacity also placed limitations on the study. It was necessary that I distance myself from the information that I knew as a result of being a reentry professional and as a former staff member of the community helping agency.

Conclusion

A convergence of several legal, societal and political developments has resulted in a dramatic increase in both the number of people being incarcerated and the average length of incarceration in America. More specifically, the number of females being incarcerated is at an all-time high in this country. Regardless of the cause of these spiraling incarceration statistics, the results are the same. The number of families impacted by incarceration has increased dramatically resulting in family systems being severely stressed and mandating that family scientists; practitioners, researchers, and others find new and more effective ways to address this growing problem (Arditti, Lambert-Shute, & Joest; (2003).

Ethically, morally, nor economically can this country afford not to embrace reentry. Moreover cannot afford to embrace the importance of reentry as an important subsystem for family stabilization, neighborhood revitalization or community development.

Incarceration has been conceptualized as a disruptive process for both individuals and families associated with significant losses (Arditti, Lambert-Shute, & Joest; (2003). These losses are broadly categorized into two categories: economic and social relationships. Family dynamics are often shifted creating a temporary, involuntary single parent household or a kinship care scenario. While some incarcerated parents were not the primary care providers at the time of incarceration, it still impacts every family (Arditti, Lambert-Shute, & Joest; (2003).

The stigma associated with incarceration is also a significant factor that impacts both the incarcerated individual and the family. Often the stigma associated with incarceration is not perceived nor treated like other kinds of losses for families, such as death, divorce or absence due to military service, resulting in further separation from supportive services and individuals (Arditti, Lambert-Shute, & Joest; (2003).

Reentry is a necessary part of the rebuilding process for both families and communities. While the number of females who are incarcerated remains less than the numbers of males who are incarcerated, the rate of female incarceration is dramatically increasing. With the number of female, single parent households increasing in this country, the impact of female incarceration and the issue of female reentry increases in significance. The viabilities of families are substantially impacted by the female ex-offender barriers. If the family as well as the incarcerated individual is to recover from the family member's incarceration then the barriers impacting successful reentry and reintegration must be explored further and addressed in a more holistic manner.

(Table 1)

Demographics of Sample

Had resided in a therapeutic community before release	Residing in Therapeutic Community at time of interview	Not- Residing in Therapeutic Community at time of Interview	Had previously resided in a therapeutic community after release
3	3	4	2
	African American 3	Caucasian 4	
unemployed at time of interview 2	Employed at time of interview 5	Secured employment through networking 4	Secured employment Without use of referral or networking 1

38

Interview Questions

1. Since your release and reentry into the Community, what has your experience been with employment opportunities?

2. What has been your experience since your release from incarceration with identifying educational opportunities?

3. Since your release from incarceration and reentry into the Community, what has been your experience concerning your family relationships (including marital relations, if applicable)?

4. What has been your experience since your release from incarceration with associations and social interactions?

5. What has been your experience since your release from incarceration with substance abuse?

6. Since your release from incarceration and reentry into the Community, what has been your experience with community functioning?

7. What has been your experience since your release from incarceration with personal and emotional orientation (this would include your behavior, how you think, and problem-solving skills)?

8. Since your release from incarceration and reentry into the Community, what has been your experience with attitude, your own attitude and the attitudes of others you encounter (those you encounter regularly and also infrequent or incidental encounters)?

(Appendix B)

Criminogenic Needs

A lot of research in the past twenty years has amply demonstrated that certain types of correctional programs have been clearly shown to be more effective in reducing recidivism. In predicting recidivism, we know that there are a number of "static" factors that are predictive. These are factors such as age, juvenile and adult criminal history, etc. Programming cannot change these static factors, but it can address other predictive factors that influence an offender's current behavior, values, and attitudes. These areas, which a) have been shown to be associated with recidivism and b) can be changed, are called *criminogenic needs*. Which dynamic factors are actually criminogenic needs and which are not does not always match some of the commonly held perceptions and beliefs of corrections staff (Retrieved November 16, 2009, from http://www.drc.ohio.gov/web/ipp_criminogenic.htm.).

Ohio Department of Rehabilitation and Correction last updated March 16, 2006.

References

Arditti, J.A. & Few, A.L., (2006). Mothers" reentry into family life following incarceration. *Criminal Justice Policy Review, 17*(1), 103-123.

Bailey, C.A. (2007). *A guide to qualitative field research, second edition.* Thousand Oaks, CA: Pine Forge Press.

Bredehoft, D. J, & Walcheski, M. J. (2003). Internal dynamics of families. In D. J. Bredehoft & M. J. Walcheski (Eds.), Family life education: Integrating theory and practice (pp.68-74). Minneapolis, MN: National Council on Family Relations.

Boss, P. (1999). *Ambiguous loss: Learning to live with unresolved grief.* Cambridge, MA: Harvard University Press.

Bush, G.W., (2004). Faith-Based and Community Initiatives-Prisoner Re-Entry Initiative. Retrieved September 17, 2007, from *http://www.whitehouse.gov/news/releases/2004/01/20040123-4.html.* 01/23/04 - Fact Sheet: Seeking Fair Treatment for Faith-Based and Community Charities *...georgewbush-whitehouse.archives.gov/government/.../factsheet.html*

Chibucos, T.R. & Leite, R.W., (2005). *Readings in Family Theory,* Thousand Oaks, CA: Sage.

Creswell, J.W. (2003). *Research design qualitative, quantitative, and mixed measures approaches, second edition.* Thousand Oaks, CA: Sage Publications, Inc.

Elsner, A. (2004). *Gates of injustice: The crisis in America's prisons.* Upper Saddle River, NJ: FT Prentice Hall.

Golden, R. (2005). *War on the family: mothers in prison and the families they leave behind.* New York: Routledge.

Gonnerman, J. (2004). *Life on the outside: The prison odyssey of Elaine Bartlett.* New York: Farrar, Straus, and Giroux.

Herman, R., Osiris, K., & Villa, A. (2004). The *Psychology of incarceration: A distortion of the state of belonging.* Beavercreek, OH: Hanbleceya House, Inc.

Locke, L.F., Spirduso, W.W., & Silverman, S.J. (2000). *Proposals that work, 4th ed.* Thousand Oaks, CA: Sage.

Minuchin, P. (1985). Families and individual development: Provocations from the
field of family therapy. *Child Development, 56*(2), 289-302.

Mullis, R.L., Brailsford, J.C., & Mullis, A.K. (2005). Relations between identity
formation and family characteristics among young adults. In T.R. Chibucos &
R.W. Leite (Eds.), *Readings in Family Theory* (pp. 282-292). Thousand Oaks,
CA: Sage.

Mumola, C.J., Bureau of Justice Statistics Special Report. (2000). *Incarcerated
parents and their children*. Retrieved September 17, 2007, from
http://www.ojp.usdoj.gov/bjs/abstract/iptc.htm.

O'Brien, P. (2001). Making *it in the "free world": Women in transition from prison.*
Albany, NY: State University of New York Press.

Ohio Department of Rehabilitation and Correction. (March 16, 2006). *Criminogenic
Needs* Retrieved November 15, 2009, from
http://www.drc.ohio.gov/web/ipp_criminogenic.htm.

Osher, F.C. (2007). Short-term strategies to improve reentry of jail populations:
Expanding and implementing the APIC model. *American Jails,
January/February*, 1-8.

Petersilia, J. (2003). *When prisoners come home: Parole and prisoner reentry.*
Studies in crime and public policy. Oxford: Oxford University Press.

Poehlmann, J., (2005). Representations of attachment relationships in children of
incarcerated mothers. *Child Development, 76*(3), 679-696.

Reisig, M.D., Bales, W.D., Hay, C., & Wang, X. (2007). The effect of racial inequality
on black male recidivism. *Justice Quarterly, 24*(3), 408-434.

Travis, J. (2000). *But they all come back: Rethinking prisoner reentry.* Washington,
DC: National Institute of Justice.

Travis, J., & Visher, C. A. (2005). *Prisoner reentry and crime in America.*
Cambridge: Cambridge University Press.

Travis, J., & Waul, M. (2003). *Prisoners once removed: The impact of incarceration and
reentry on children, families, and communities.* Washington, D.C.: Urban Institute
Press.

U.S. Department of Justice Office of Justice Programs (2004). *Reentry.* Retrieved
    September 17, 2007 from, http://www.reentry.gov/learn.html.

Visher, C., & Travis, J. (2003). Transitions from prison to community: Understanding
    individual pathways. *Annual Review of Sociology, 29*(1), 89-113.

Warren, C.A.B. & Karner, T.X. (2005). Discovering qualitative methods. Los
    Angeles: Roxbury.

Western, B. (2006). *Punishment and inequality in America.* New York: Russell Sage.

White, J.M., & Klein, D.M. (2002). Family *theories, 2nd ed.,* Thousand Oaks, CA:
    Sage.

Lightning Source UK Ltd.
Milton Keynes UK
UKOW03f0152070617
302829UK00001B/108/P